C000149282

SETH ROGEN

Table of Contents

Introduction

One of the most popular comedy actors of the 21st century, Seth Rogen is much more than the goofy men he portrays in movies. Getting his start in Hollywood on the short-lived cult TV show *Freak and* Geeks, Rogen developed a friendship with the director, Judd Apatow. This proved to be a fortuitous friendship for Rogan's career. Apatow encouraged him to try to get parts on the big screen. Rogan's career quickly took off after he landed a role as the lead actor in the film *Knocked Up*, which received critical and commercial acclaim and success. His charming, laid-back persona, coupled with a unique laugh, helped launch him into the comedic spotlight. Having worked with a friend to draft *Superbad* when he was only thirteen years old, he has become recognized as a multi-talented comedian. Although he has worked behind the scenes as a writer since the end of *Freaks and Geeks*, Rogan has moved behind the camera as a director and a producer.

Using his platform and persona, Rogen began to champion causes that he felt were important. He has become a vocal advocate of legalizing marijuana. He even started his own Cannabis company, Houseplant. As soon as his website launched in March of 2021, it received so much traffic that it crashed the site. He has also deeply committed to raising awareness and promoting research into Alzheimer's Disease. He even testified before the US Congress about the illness and the need for more Alzheimer's research funding. He and his wife began the Hilarity for Charity movement to bring greater awareness of the disease to the public. They also provide support for families who are affected by the ailment.

Chapter 1

Early Life

On April 15, 1982, Sandy Rogen gave birth to her and her husband's second child, Seth Aaron Rogen. The family was close-knit. Seth's mother was a social worker in Vancouver, and his father was an employee at the nonprofit BC Coalition of People with Disabilities. His parents raised Seth and his sister in a liberal Jewish environment, encouraging them to do things that they love in their comfortable home in Vancouver, British Columbia. His education was typical for children in the family's area, with the young Rogen going to Vancouver Talmud Torah Elementary for his early education and Point Grey Secondary School for his last years of schooling. Though they lived in Canada, Rogen's father was American, and Rogen became a dual citizen (US/Canadian) when he was ten years old.

Seth knew from an early age that making people laugh was what he wanted to do for a living. He started doing stand-up comedy around the

Vancouver comedy circuit when he was just 12 years old. Many of the other comedians were a decade older than he was. Clips of some of his earliest appearances are still available to entertain people online, and some of his jokes were a good bit more mature than his age. He also talked about what it was like to grow up Jewish, satirizing the experience in a crowd-pleasing way. Though there appears to be some nervous energy when he first starts talking, it quickly shifts to amusement from the audience as his jokes continue to land with audiences. One of his early appearances was filmed in 1994 when he appeared at The Lotus.

Looking like a typical "skater kid" with a mop-top, the young Rogen was able to keep the room entertained for nearly 10 minutes, using material that was decidedly from the perspective of a child, but with a much older spin. For example, he once opened with, "Well, hi. I'm Seth Rogen and I'd like to tell you a bit about myself. I'm a two-time *Playgirl* centerfold. No, not really. But I am *Jewish*." From an early age, he knew how to flip expectations. He would state something obviously false, then follow it up with something unrelated. This exercise in absurdity made people laugh and helped to put his audiences at ease, letting them know that he could hold his own up on stage despite his youth.

Seth may have inherited a funny gene from his mother. She has maintained a very active presence on Twitter, and her random tweets are just as startling, jarring, and funny as Rogen's early comedy appearances.

Comedy was not Rogen's only interest while he was growing up. He took karate classes, and he attributes the lessons learned in those classes for his resilience. He was one of about two dozen kids in his karate class when he started. Three years later, he was the only one who was still going. Everyone else had dropped out - and he was the best of a new batch of kids. As he pointed out, it was his ability to keep going, to not give up, that helped him finish at the top of the class. To him, that was the critical lesson that taught him about perseverance. Given his chosen field, this was instrumental in his outlook on finding success.

When he eventually started to get roles in film and TV, he often played the part of a laid back, goofy, low achiever. This was not the person he was, though. He admitted that he has actually worked very hard. He learned that working hard was one of the few things about any situation that he could control. If everything else worked out, great, but at least he always knew that he was working toward the goal.

When he was just 16 years old, Rogen won the Vancouver Amateur Comedy Contest, giving him the push he needed for his first major change in his life. After receiving the award, Rogen decided to drop out of high school and move to Los Angeles to pursue a career in comedy.

Chapter 2

Moving to LA

Rogen received a casting call for an upcoming TV show that was to be directed by Judd Apatow in the late 1990s. The aspiring actor went through two auditions for the part of the teenager, Ken, in a show called *Freaks and Geeks*. The character was described as a burnout with an ascorbic sense of humor, which significantly defined and differentiated the character from the other teenagers on the show.

The cast was comprised of a host of teenage actors. By the time filming started, Rogen was 17. Compared to his entertaining and affable persona on the stages in Vancouver, he played a much more stubborn and sarcastic character in the show. Ken's character was from a wealthier family. He was even raised by a nanny, which made Ken notably different from most of his friends. His life goals revolved around inheriting his father's company, then turning around and selling it off so that he could retire to an easy life.

In addition to being Rogen's first television role, the show jump-started several remarkable actors, including Samm Levine, Jason Segel, James Franco, and Busy Phillips. Many of the cast members went on to work together, but Rogen and Franco maintained a close friendship over the years, acting in numerous movies together.

Freaks and Geeks focused on a group of teens who lived in a suburb of Detroit. Apatow wanted the show to look gloomy and cold, setting the show apart from many other teenagers' shows, like *Dawson's Creek,* that were popular at the time. The lighting was adjusted to create a gloomier tone, with gray and green tinting to hide the fact that the show was actually filmed in sunny California. The show's soundtrack included many popular songs, consuming a large chunk of the budget. Since most of the actors in the show were new to the entertainment industry, the network did not need to pay unknown actors as much as other professionals. However, the show was unique, and it was a phenomenal springboard for many of the cast. Instead of focusing on popular teens or cool kids, the show was about a bunch of socially invisible kids who were slightly mischievous - without being "bad boys" or "bad girls" in their schools. Many of the *Freaks and Geeks* actors were encouraged to do some of their own writing. Franco was brought into a brainstorming session to see how Apatow and other creators of the show handled the process of getting their ideas on paper. Segel and Rogen both spent some of their time keeping up their own comedy routines and writing their own jokes over the weekends. This was when Rogen began to consider the script he had worked on earlier, making changes to the early draft to make it a lot closer to the script for *Superbad*.

Even though the cast worked well together, the exceptional talent of the actors gained a great deal of attention for the show. It was critically acclaimed, but NBC put it in one of the most unpopular time slots. The show first aired at a relatively unpopular television time slot - 8 pm on Saturday, September 25, 1999. When the World Series began in October, *Freaks and Geeks* was taken off the air so that people could watch baseball instead. When NBC resumed airing the show, they put the show during a time that competed with *Who Wants to Be a Millionaire*, a top-rated show at the time. To bring more attention to the show, the producers created a website, in part to let audiences know when the show was going to be on air next. Despite the producers' efforts, NBC did not provide the site's URL in their ads.

It did not take long before most of the people involved in the show knew that there would not be a second season of the show. Paul Feig wrote the last episode knowing that it would be the last, ensuring that the characters got enough of a sendoff so that the show's fans would have some closure. Despite the critical acclaim that the show received, even winning an Emmy for Outstanding Casting in a Comedy Series, the show did not get renewed for a second season.

With his first big acting gig wrapped up, Rogen had many options for his path forward, especially with his friendship with Apatow. This was a springboard for a much bigger career.

Chapter 3

Judd Apatow

Apatow has admitted that much of his career, following the cancellation of *Freaks and Geeks,* was a sort of revenge against the TV network that had seemed to undermine the show's chance at succeeding. Part of that revenge entailed helping the actors in the show to find success. They were talented actors and had been recognized for their abilities by the people who awarded the Emmys. Following the show's ending, Apatow went on to direct *40 Year Old Virgin*. Over the next few years, he returned again and again to the *Freaks and Geeks* actors.

While Apatow was looking for revenge through success, he encouraged the actors to try bigger and better things. He encouraged Rogen to look to film for his next big project. However, Rogen appeared on several unsuccessful shows before reaching that point. Rogen wrote for the *Da Ali G Show*, starring Sacha Baron Cohen, working for the show during the second and final season.

Although the show did not do particularly well in the ratings, some of the people who were behind the scenes did get more media attention, notably Cohen as Borat and Bruno; each became titular characters in Cohen's later movies. Rogen also appeared in an episode of the popular teen drama *Dawson's Creek*.

Apatow had been impressed by how comfortable Rogen was in front of the camera, especially as it was the first time he had been on a show, speaking someone else's words. Rogen was allowed to use some of his own jokes, and he impressed the director. He had a bit part in the cult classic movie *Donnie Darko*, then was in another short-lived TV show called *Undeclared*, another Apatow sitcom. It went on to become another cult classic.

When Apatow began to work on films, he hired Rogen, first with a small part in the well-received *Anchorman: The Legend of Ron Burgundy*. The movie was released in 2004. However, in 2005, Rogen gained much more attention when he got a more prominent role in the movie *The 40-Year-Old Virgin*. The movie featured a host of funny actors, including Steve Carell, but when Rogen was on screen, his wit and delivery often ended up stealing scenes. This was the first time he worked with Paul Rudd and Jonah Hill, two men who have become closely associated with Rogen's career and projects. Despite his relatively minor role in the film, he was credited as a co-producer of the popular comedy. Rogen had another supporting role in the comedy, *You, Me, and Dupree*.

Rogen's resilience came in handy when he was looking for more consistent work. He spent more time writing as he was not finding much success as an actor. He auditioned for parts in *Eternal Sunshine of the Spotless Mind* and *The Office*. After three years of more minor roles, Rogen was given his breakout role in another Apatow film, *Knocked Up*.

Chapter 4

Success

After a few years of spending as much time writing as acting, Rogen finally landed his first lead role in another Apatow movie - *Knocked Up*. His character, Ben Stone, was a Canadian slacker who was able to get the attractive, professional Alison Scott to spend the night with him. The one-night stand turns into something much more serious when she discovers that she is pregnant. Suddenly forced to face an unplanned reality, Ben wanted to be an active part of the child's life, despite an increasingly contentious relationship with Alison.

He lived with several slacker roommates, played by Segel (from *Freaks and Geeks*), Martin Star, Jay Baruchel, and Jonah Hill. The actors bonded on the set, and the director invited them over to his place to improvise the scenes. They tried to develop different ways to make the interactions more interesting, and Seth Goldberg, one of Rogen's writing companions, suggested that they play the "Dirty Man Competition." Goldberg described the challenge to the director, saying, "We'd have a bet with a guy to see how long he could go without shaving or showering or cutting his hair." Segal further added that "We thought we could chart the nine months based on Martin's beard length." This helped the actors to build a more natural rapport with each other, which translated well on the screen.

Knocked Up was also the first acting role for Ken Jeong, who, at the time, was on vacation from his job as a doctor, and later starred in many more hit movies, including *The Hangover* and *Crazy Rich Asians*. The creators and cast of *Knocked Up* had fun making the movie (except for co-star Katherine Heigl, who let her dislike of the film be known soon after its release, calling the movie "A little sexist"), and the movie was both critically and commercially successful. Although he was an unconventional leading man, Rogen showed that he had the charisma and ability to hold his own against other, well-known actors, and he quickly became a highly bankable actor. With *Knocked Up*, Rogen and Apatow had managed to take a $30 million budget and turn it into a box office hit that grossed more than $220 million.

Suddenly able to take his career in whatever direction he wanted, Rogen returned to the idea that he had worked on when he was just 13 years old. Brushing off the latest version of the script for *Superbad*, Rogen began to turn the long-time dream into a reality. Originally, the script had been built more around his own ideas as a teenager, but now it had been about a decade since he first wrote it, meaning that Rogen was far too old to play one of the main characters. Jonah Hill was cast to play the role of Seth, and he brought in some improvisation from his own life that ended up in the youth vernacular.

Superbad became the first major film role for Michael Cera, who had gotten his acting start in the TV show *Arrested Development.* And it was an early role for Emma Stone too, who has gone on to become a famous actress in her own right. They also hired the *Saturday Night Live* actor Bill Hader to play one of the cops in the movie (Rogen was the other memorable police officer in the film). This was a new group of actors that went on to have substantial success in the entertainment world, fostering the kind of positive work environment that had helped nurture the talents of the cast on *Freaks and Geeks*.

Superbad has been compared to the 1980s cult classic movie *Fast Times at Ridgemont High*. It focused on the kinds of things that are important to teenagers, giving a more comedic and critical look at what drives the teenagers of the time. Like the 1980's movie, *Superbad* helped to launch several careers for young stars. The two writers wanted the movie to portray a world that was easier for teenagers to relate to, and they did it so well that the movie is still considered funny and relatable by teens years later. Following teens who have been described as dorky high schoolers trying to provide alcohol for a party in an effort to make a favorable impression on a few popular girls, the deeper problem was that the two main characters were actually nervous about the fact that their paths would soon diverge as they went to different colleges. Released in the summer of 2007, the movie received critical and commercial success. Rogen was suddenly a successful scriptwriter and could take his career in whatever direction he pleased.

Chapter 5

Overcoming

Rogen thoroughly enjoyed his post-*Superbad* success, and he took on a wide variety of projects. He lent his voice to several notable children's movies, including the following:

- *Shrek the Third*, released in 2007
- *Kung Fu Panda*, released in 2008 (as well as the two sequels)
- *Horton Hears a Who!*, released in 2008 (one of the last movies approved by Dr. Seuss's widow before her death in 2019)
- *The Spiderwick Chronicles*, released in 2008
- *Monsters vs. Aliens*, released in 2009

He also continued to write, create, and act in movies, like *Pineapple Express*, which he worked on with James Franco. The movie was released in 2008 and was met with mixed reviews, though it was still a financial success. Rogen played a stoner who teams up with his marijuana dealer after witnessing the dealer's boss murder someone. They spent the film running from hitmen. Rogen and Goldberg were the primary writers of the film. Like many of Rogen's projects, it has developed a large cult following.

That same year, Kevin Smith directed and wrote the film *Zack and Miri Make a Porno*, and it featured Rogen taking a lead acting role with Elizabeth Banks (they had both acted in *The 40-Year-Old Virgin*). In the film, two platonic childhood friends and current roommates decide to make an adult film in an effort to alleviate their financial stress, hoping to be able to use the money to pay the rent. The project ends up affecting their friendship, making it a very different kind of rom-com.

By the end of the 2000s, Rogen was one of the most bankable actors in Hollywood. In 2008, he was named the ShoWest Comedy Star of the Year, and he was named the Canadian Comedy Person of the Year in both 2008 and 2009.

His first big role in the 2010s was meant to be a superhero blockbuster, *The Green Hornet*. He worked with his long-term writing partner, Evan Goldberg. Later, Rogen described the decision by saying that they "fell into the trap … when you start doing well, you inherent[ly] gravitate towards the notion of doing the biggest thing that you can, basically." They began working without understanding the full weight of what a big-budget movie entails. It was the first time that they had far less control in what was happening as investors and others who helped to fund the project wanted more control than any other project that Rogen had been on. It was also a very different kind of movie than Rogen and Goldberg had done before, and the actor has said that a part of the problem with his work on the movie was the hubris that he brought to it after having nearly a decade of successes. He called the experience a nightmare. With so much studio interference, they could not create the kind of film they had envisioned. The script required many reworks to satisfy everyone, and there were certain expectations about family and plot that the studio tried to force into the film. It took the crew three years to make the movie, and Rogen expressed how he and the core group were annoyed, saying "We could've made five movies in that time.

Rogen was quick to affirm, however, that their studio, Sony, remained supportive for the duration of the project. When the movie was poorly received and widely panned, Rogen and the team were not held responsible because the studio, investors, and others had played a significant role in the end product.

He was a part of another project released in 2011. Working with two famous British comedians, Simon Pegg and Nick Frost, Rogen voiced the titular alien in the sci-fi comedy, *Paul*. The character was much more aligned with Rogen's onscreen persona as the alien was quick-witted and unconventional.

The Green Hornet was a lesson that Rogen and his colleagues learned from, and they went back to being the people who did what they wanted to do on a much smaller budget – the people that were "getting away with a lot of really cool stuff," instead of being the people with a large budget and all of the unwelcome focus. *The Green Hornet* was his first career failure, and he has made sure not to be put under that kind of scrutiny again. He worked with Barbra Streisand in the comedy *The Guilt Trip,* released in 2012, showing that he still had plenty of influence in Hollywood and could be a draw for other talents. He also worked with Will Reiser (they had previously worked on *Da Ali G Show* writing for Sacha Baron Cohen) to write and produce a recounting of Reiser's experience with cancer. The result was the movie *50/50*. Joseph Gordon-

Levitt played a 27-year-old Adam Lerner who learned that he had a potentially terminal form of cancer. Rogen played the part of his friend, who helps Lerner get through the challenges and cope with the diagnosis. It also reflects some of Reisner and Rogen's actual relationships in real life. Though the movie is a comedy, it has a lot more raw emotion than was typical for most of Rogen's previous movies. Reisner admitted that it was not entirely true to life, but it was a realistic look at what patients and their loved ones go through when dealing with cancer.

Rogen and his friends did another self-parody in what has been described as an apocalyptic comedy, *This Is the End*. The seeds for the movie started years earlier when he and Baruchel worked on a much shorter script, *Jay and Seth Versus the Apocalypse*. This movie was a unique kind of movie, and it marked Rogen's debut as a director.

He has maintained a relatively steady stream of successful comedies with *Neighbors (2014)* and its sequel. He also worked on Franco's project *The Sound and the Fury* (an adaptation of the William Faulkner tale) and the satirical movie *Sausage Party*. They had learned their lesson from *The Green Hornet*. Now, they wanted to get as much money from the studios as possible and then have the studios go away and let them focus on doing what they wanted with as little oversight as possible. They would ensure that they would be able to do this more freely by founding their own small studio.

Chapter 6

Personal Life

Rogen has always been open about his life, from growing up in Canada to his enjoyment of marijuana. In fact, much of his personal life has been built into his characters and helped make people feel like they know him better than they actually do.

Like many actors, though, the person that people know on screen is not exactly who Rogen really is. As funny and entertaining as he seems to be, Rogen takes many aspects of his personal life very seriously. He has attributed his style and humor to being Canadian and Jewish. Goldberg and Rogen met at a bar mitzvah class, and they got along well. When they realized that they would be going their separate ways in high school, they got the idea for the movie *Superbad*. As soon as Rogen could turn his early script into a movie, he did. He once said that part of the idea came from the fact that other guys would be flirting with the female students, but not Rogen and his high school friends – they were standing around joking and smoking marijuana. It was essentially practice for his career. Looking back, Rogen once said during an interview that finding out that people were paid to be funny as a career was all he needed to hear to know that was the profession for him.

While working as a writer for the *Da Ali G Show*, Rogen met Lauren Miller in 2004. The show was in its last season, so they did not work together for long, but they continued to talk and were dating within a year. Seven years later, they married in October 2011. Miller still writes, but she also acts and directs, staying as busy as her husband. He even cast her in small parts for a couple of his movies, including *Superbad*. They celebrated their nine years of marriage in 2020, with the actor expressing his happiness at the occasion, saying he had found "the perfect partner to go through life." The celebratory tone quickly shifted to his brand of humor. As he said he was falling in love with her more every day, even after nine years of marriage, he showed "proof" of his love by adding an image with the description, "Here's me beating her at video games at our wedding." Apart from the occasional posts, they keep their relationship private.

Rogen has often reflected on the differences between Canada and the United States. Things like marijuana use and same-sex marriage were issues that had already been resolved in Canada, so it was different to hear the subjects still being debated in the US. When same-sex marriage finally became legal in the US in June 2015, Rogen became active in supporting the decision. Just a year after the US Supreme Court ruling, he and fellow comedian Amy Schumer accepted roles in a Bud Light commercial featuring a male couple getting married (they were wedding guests). As a representative for Bud Light explained, "By featuring Seth and Amy at a same-sex wedding, we're showing how all weddings – regardless of who is getting married - share many similarities and moments to celebrate."

Rogen actually suffers from a mild case of Tourette's Syndrome, which he has openly discussed on Twitter. In January 2021, when US Senator Ted Cruz tried to take on the comedian after the US re-committed to the Paris Climate Agreement, he attempted to make light of the disease to insult Rogen. To the attempted insult, Rogen responded, "As someone who has Tourette's in their family (and also has a very mild case himself), I once again take great pleasure in telling you to go f*** yourself. (Also, VERY few cases of Tourette's manifest in uncontrollable swearing. Most cases, like mine, manifest in twitching." He was able to not only use the stereotype of a serious disease to insult the senator, but he was also able to use the platform to provide some real information about the problem. It is this more personable approach that often makes him so popular with younger generations. He never used the medical condition as an excuse for not succeeding, and until the first month of 2021, he had never mentioned it.

Chapter 7

Controversies

As with any celebrity who speaks openly about their views, Rogen has found himself in several controversies. Some might point to a movie like *Sausage Party*, which has been interpreted as a critique of religion, or movies that normalize marijuana (several years before any US states legalized it for recreational use), but it has been things that he has said outside of his acting career that has drawn the most controversy.

However, there was one movie that gained much attention and courted controversy in a way that created some international tensions. Rogen and Goldberg wrote and directed the movie *The Interview*, with Rogen and Franco starring in it. It was meant to be a comedy with Rogen acting as a producer and Franco as a tabloid reporter who gets a chance to interview the North Korean dictator Kim Jong-un. This was probably the kind of movie that he had meant in his remarks after the difficult experience with *The Green Hornet*.

Sony was again the studio that backed the movie, but when North Korea learned of the subject matter – the two leads were given a mission to assassinate the dictator – they threatened to take action against the movie studio. The movie may not have had a blockbuster budget, but international threats did draw attention to the smaller movie. A short time after North Korea's threat, Sony Pictures was hacked, and there was a large leak of a lot of the company's private data that was made available to the public. The company suspected that it was North Korea that ordered the hack. Eventually, the movie's release was canceled because no major theater would show it. A few independent theaters did show the movie at the time. All of the interest and controversy about the movie ensured that people would seek it out through other means. Now it is available on different streaming services, as well as being on Blu-ray and DVD.

Perhaps the most notable controversy associated with Rogen's personal life is his open criticism of Israel, saying that he and other Jewish children had been "fed a huge amount of lies about Israel." During the interview on a podcast, he said a number of things that made people question whether or not he was serious, especially as he seemed to say that there was no need for Israel to exist. He later went on to say that much of what he said was not serious, then acknowledged that "It's a tricky conversation to have in jest. My pride in being Jewish and how deeply I identify as a Jewish person perhaps made me feel like I was able to say things without as much context as perhaps I should have given them." While he did not mean much of what he said, he still seemed critical of what Jewish students are told. His actual view is not very easy to determine because it is difficult to tell when he is being serious. He has joked about being Jewish for decades, so it is very likely harder for him to discuss it in a way that is devoid of humor. He does take the persecution of Jewish people around the world seriously, and he has spoken out against the rise of anti-Semitism, but he likely does have some criticisms as there is usually a grain of sincerity in his jokes.

Rogen and many of his friends and colleagues are among the cult following of the infamously terrible movie *The Room* by Tommy Wiseau, which was released in 2003. The movie is often described as being so terrible that it might be good. It has been described as one of the worst movies ever made, but the choices made were strange, and the end product is humorous on its own. The movie has earned a large cult following, and Rogen and his friends decided to make a movie about the making of *The Room*. They called their film *The Disaster Artist*, after the non-fiction book by Greg Sestero about his experience in working in the movie. Their movie was released in 2017 and starred Franco as the actor Wiseau. He was also the director of the film, just as Wiseau had been. Rogen took on the role of script supervisor in the movie. Their movie had a much better reception, receiving nominations for awards from the Screen Actors Guild and the Golden Globes. In early 2018, several students who had attended Franco's acting classes joined in the *Me Too* movement, alleging that the star had acted inappropriately with them. The sexual misconduct allegations meant that the movie was scrutinized because of its director/actor, so Franco stopped going to the different award shows that recognized what the film had accomplished. Other people from the production attended the ceremonies instead. This was not a controversy that Rogen was directly responsible for, but because of the timing of the film's release and his close friendship with Franco, it brought more scrutiny on the project.

Not all of his controversies have been nearly so serious, though. During the MTV Movie Awards in 2008, Rogen was promoting *Pineapple Express* with Franco. The pair had brought a joint onstage, and they lit it, causing the cameras to cut away from them and their antics. They explained that it was to show off what their characters were like, further plugging the movie. As Rogen pointed out, everything they said during their time on stage was written down on the teleprompter. Since all of their actions were planned and predictable based on the script, it was argued that the blame was not entirely on them.

There have also been instances when he and his friends seemed to court controversy, like with their TV show *Preacher*. The show was based on a controversial comic book series, all but guaranteeing they would face backlash for the show's content. It took them two seasons to successfully offend enough people to face backlash, particularly from Christians.

Given his comedic history, sense of humor, and enthusiasm for marijuana, there will likely be many more controversies, though many of them will probably be on the provocative side.

Chapter 8

Activism

Rogen may play well-meaning slackers and goofballs on screen, but he is still every bit the hardworking man who headed to LA when he was young. That hard work includes his efforts for causes about which he is passionate.

The cause that he is best known for is his work get marijuana legalized in the United States (the 2018 *Cannabis Act* made marijuana legal everywhere in Canada). Taking his typical approach, he says that he wants to keep fighting "America's racist policies in regards to weed." The way he words his thinking about the use of marijuana is somewhat humorous, but it is based on statistics that show that the legal system does not treat all people the same way when they are arrested for possession of weed. As Rogen has pointed out, it disproportionately affects minorities and tends to punish them more severely. He says he does not want to "shy away from very uncomfortable conversations," as his career and outspoken personality has repeatedly demonstrated. He continued, saying that he and the people he works with will "always do whatever we can to remind people that currently there are people in jail in America for weed, and there are people whose lives are being ruined by weed."

Another cause important to Rogen is raising awareness about Alzheimer's Disease. A year after they started to date, Miller's mother was told that she was in the early stages of Alzheimer's. This was Rogen's first time seeing the disease up close, and it left him wanting to do more to help combat it. However, if he were going to take on something as serious and devastating as the degenerative disease, he would do it on his own terms.

According to the Alzheimer's Association, the disease is the "most common cause of dementia, a general term for memory loss and the loss of other cognitive abilities that are serious enough to interfere with daily life. Alzheimer's disease accounts for 60-80% of dementia cases." The disease tends to affect people over 65, but more aggressive versions can begin to affect a person's mind while in their 40s, with roughly 200,000 Americans suffering from early-onset Alzheimer's, meaning patients are under 65 years old. This is the group that Miller's mother fell into when she was diagnosed. People who have the disease can live for more than 20 years after the diagnosis, but the problem is that they will begin to lose their memories and their sense of self over time. Their mental abilities continue to decline with time, so that when the patients reach the later stages, they often cannot carry on a conversation and can even lose the ability to react to their surroundings. In the worst cases, they will not even remember who they are by the time they die. There are many things linked to the disease, such as chronic sleep deprivation, but there is no known cure for the disease, and researchers are still trying to determine the causes. Some treatments can help slow the disease, but it does not prevent the steady degradation of the patient's quality of life.

Seeing someone suffering from the disease can be unbelievably difficult, and it inspired Rogen to do all that he could to help. In 2012, he and his new wife started Hilarity for Charity (HFC). The HFC's "mission is to care for families impacted by Alzheimer's disease, inspire the next generation of Alzheimer's advocates, and be leaders in brain health research and education."

They have drawn in many other prominent celebrities to help support that mission, and they regularly hold events to raise awareness and get donations to help in the research against Alzheimer's. They organized a Netflix special that included some of the biggest names in comedy at the time, such as Tiffany Haddish, Sacha Baron Cohen, and Michael Che.

In 2014, Rogen testified before the US Congress about Alzheimer's and the lack of funding available to fight the disease. He did add a little humor, beginning by saying, "First, I should answer the question I assume many of you are asking. Yes, I'm aware this has nothing to do with the legalization of marijuana." His testimony then quickly turned serious as he highlighted the sharp decline that he had witnessed in his mother-in-law. Once he was done talking, Rogen took to Twitter to call out - by name - the 16 Senators who walked out or failed to show up for the important discussion. It was one of the few times that his tweets were devoid of humor. He was upset by the disengagement of the people who were supposed to represent Americans, especially on a subject that affects hundreds of thousands of Americans every year.

Miller's mother died in 2020, living 15 years after her initial diagnosis, but she was the second person that Miller had seen slowly deteriorate from the disease; she had seen her grandmother slowly decline and die from it before her mother received the diagnosis. Seeing his mother-in-law deteriorate, Rogen said, "With Laruen's mother, it went very dark very fast. It was devoid of humor in every way, shape, or form." His wife had a much better idea of what was coming, and she knew to focus on what she could control.

Chapter 9

Business

Rogen found a way to do more than advocate for the legalization of marijuana. He decided to turn his interest into another job. Working again with his long-term writing partner Goldberg, they started the company Houseplant. According to his Twitter announcement in March 2021, he had been considering starting a weed company for about a decade.

The company's "goal is to be the most thoughtful weed company in the world. That means considering every detail to give reverence to the plant that's been a part of our daily lives for over 20 years." There is a lot more to the website than just selling their products. They have an entire section dedicated to educating people about what marijuana does, how to safely consume it, and much other information about other elements of the product. As their website mission statement concludes, "We just love weed so much. It's unlike anything on earth, and it's proudly made us the people we are today, which is why we work tirelessly to be the company that weed deserves."

The duo officially launched their company in March of 2019 in Canada, soon after weed was made legal all across Canada. It was meant to be a global company that provided cannabis and hemp to anywhere that the sale was legal. They both expressed how pleased they were to be bringing a product they loved to people in their home country. The company is based out of Toronto, Canada. While Rogen had been thinking about it for a decade, the two had been actively working on the project for more than five years before the company was finally launched. Their first available product was Houseplant Sativa, which became available in the early part of April 2019. They soon began to add other strains of the plant to their inventory.

Two years later, Rogen announced on Twitter that they would start selling weed to people in the US. Rogen went online to announce the move on March 1, 2021, saying that Houseplant would begin by selling to residents of his adopted home state of California. The states of Washington and Colorado made consumption of marijuana legal during 2012; Washington, DC, and Oregon legalized recreational use in 2014. California, Nevada, and Massachusetts legalized in 2016. Whatever the reason, they opted to sell only to California residents for their initial sales in the US.

Their site went live soon after the announcement, and there was so much traffic to it that the site crashed the same day. The entrepreneurs made sure to let their customers know that their products were still available – they just needed to get the site set up so that it could handle the massive influx of traffic. Rogen tweeted out the explanation saying, "Well...we have underestimated you once again. Due to insane traffic, we took the Houseplant site down temporarily while I learn to write code." It was a mix of his usual humor with enough information to put people at ease. It took a few hours, but the site was back up later the same day.

Though the company is still young, it is being launched in the early days of marijuana legalization. With two well-known people at the helm, it could become a formidable player in the burgeoning market.

Chapter 10

Future

Looking to the future, Rogen has many paths to new success available to him. He also remains heavily invested in his charity work and in helping his friends with their careers. For example, following the success of *Superbad*, one of the lead actors, Jonah Hill, had the chance to join the large blockbuster series *Transformers*, but Rogen advised him against it, saying, "I can see if Steven Spielberg's calling you, asking you to do something, how that's hard to turn down. You want to make a movie about fightin' robots? Make your own movie about fightin' robots. You can do that. That's on the table now." Instead of moving into one of the *Transformer* sequels, Hill did a cameo in the comedy *Night at the Museum 2*.

Rogen will continue to work with HFC, coming up with new ways to bring awareness and research to Alzheimer's, and he will continue developing his marijuana company. Typically, he does not give much warning about what he is working on, announcing projects just before their release. There may be other projects on the horizon, though it is difficult to imagine that he will have much time for another major undertaking.

He and Goldberg started their own Canadian production company in 2011, Point Grey Pictures, named after their secondary school where the pair met and started working together. Between 2011 and 2020, they only made 13 movies, but following the Covid-19 lockdown of 2020 and 2021, they began to pick up on their brainstorming. Every week, the 13 employees of the company watched a designated movie, then teleconferenced to discuss those movies. They produce independent films that are well outside the usual fare on the screen. The following are some of the most notable projects in development.

- Point Grey Partners is working with Nickelodeon to make an animated movie based on the popular 1990s TV show *Teenage Mutant Ninja Turtles*.
- *Cobweb* is a film adaptation of the well-known Edgar Allan Poe short story called the *Tell Tale Heart*, in which a man murders one of his

roommates, then thinks he hears the murdered man's heart beating under the floorboards where the body was hidden. They began casting for the film in the summer of 2020.

- Where's *Waldo?* is a movie that has been announced, but no synopsis has been released. The same is true for a comedy called *Not Mitzvah.*

Many other projects have been announced, but no release dates have been set.

There are some movies and shows that have been announced with thin outlines about what will be covered, such as *Bigfoot,* a made-for-TV film about the mythical creature trying to live in today's world, and *The Politician, wherein* a politician flees from the FBI only to be abducted by one of his constituents. Needless to say, Rogen will continue to be very busy for the foreseeable future.

Conclusion

Seth Rogen has been a fascinating public figure for more than two decades. Many of his early steps - like dropping out of high school to pursue a career in TV on a show that only lasted one season - would have seemed ill-advised at the time. However, he also did a lot right in the early days, learning lessons from nearly all of his experiences. It was clear early on that he was relatively fearless. After all, not many would be brave enough to step up to a mic at 13 and give a comedic spin on his young life - to an adult audience. He learned to continue to go forward even when things got difficult, which was beneficial to someone who was trying to get into film and comedy - two artistic genres that are notoriously difficult to break into. Rogen did not have a typical look that would generally make people more likely to hire him. His first job turned out to be instrumental in his overall success as he, and most of the *Freaks and Geeks* cast members, had a supportive director who was just as interested in finding success for them as for himself.

Rogen is still the same person he was at 13, stepping onto the stage in the Vancouver comedy circuit. While playing the likable slacker, he worked hard behind the scenes, taking on many different roles. He had been writing comedy for a long time, so he was able to get work writing when he did not have any acting work. This helped him to finally produce his own work and eventually move behind the camera to direct.

People know him for his work in film and TV, but he has been very active in his personal life, starting a charity for Alzheimer's research and co-founding a company associated with one of his passions, marijuana. As of 2021, his career has already been highly entertaining and unpredictable, just like his projects.

Printed in Great Britain
by Amazon